fantastic ide
for
frenzied teachers

- a survival kit for teachers of the process of writing.

Devised and illustrated by

Christine Syme.

Collins Educational

© 1986 Christine Syme

First published jointly in 1986 by
Holmes McDougall Australia and
Educational Supplies Pty Ltd., Australia.

This edition published in 1990 by Collins Educational,
London and Glasgow.

Reprinted 1991

ISBN 0 00 329475 7

Printed by Holmes McDougall Ltd., Edinburgh

In a complex information society where the mass media of communication — press, radio, television — tends to overwhelm the traditional values of originality of expression in the young, it is not surprising that teachers are increasingly stressed to produce results consistent with present community demands for a "return to literacy."

Following the continuing success of "Exciting Ideas for Frazzled Teachers", this new volume offers teachers of the writing process another valuable resource book of ideas to choose from. Not only are these ideas original and imaginative, but when activated, are guaranteed to work!

See for yourself!

Christine Syme

Writing creatively

The aim of this book is to stimulate ideas, encourage imagination and to generate originality of thought.

The process of writing cannot be regarded in isolation. All components of language — reading, writing, speaking and listening are of equal importance in developing the communicative skills of the individual. However, by expressing creativity through the written word, both process and product become an important touchstone in the pursuit of literacy goals.

The writing process comprises several distinct stages (though not every stage has to be worked through each time).

hmmm...

The desire to write

By making use of unusual or original topics it is possible to harness students' immediate interest, encourage their natural curiosity and stimulate further expression of related ideas, thoughts and feelings.

The first draft

<u>Ideas</u> are roughly jotted down , tumbled about and tossed around . The main ideas are sorted out and the form of writing is decided.

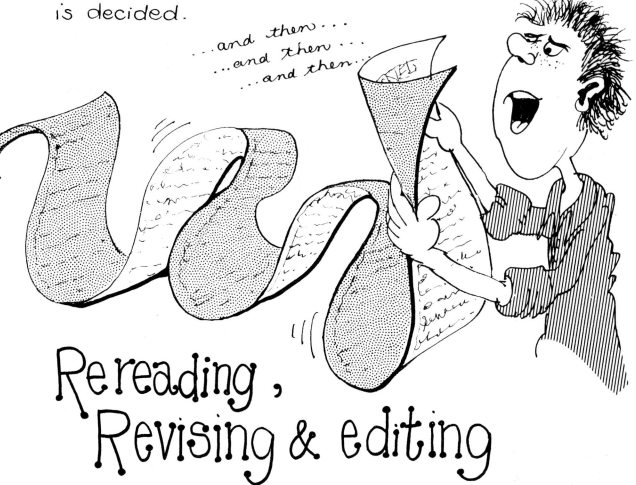

...and then...
...and then...
...and then...

Rereading ,
Revising & editing

Students critically examine their first draft — a step which involves interaction with other students and the teacher.
<u>Editing</u> is the process of re-arranging or reshuffling words and sentences.
<u>Revising</u> is the process of reviewing punctuation and improving spelling.

Final Copy & publication

Work is rewritten in preparation for presentation to an audience. Students become aware that writing can be for different audiences, including themselves, and that each audience may require different forms of publication.

Readers' response ...

Students have the opportunity to have their work read and discussed by a broad range of audiences. Audiences may include self, parents, another class, adults, the teacher, another teacher, the community. By sharing their work and gaining response, students develop an appreciation and a positive attitude towards the written word.

Invent 5 new words to programme into your robot. What does each mean?

Advertise your robot so that everyone will want to buy it.

Describe the most interesting tasks your robot can perform.

You only have a limited choice of words with which to programme your robot. List 10 words you think are the most important ones.

Your robot has written you a letter after completing many heavy tasks you assigned him. What does the letter say?

Your robot is your telephone answering service. Write down what callers will hear.

Write an ode to your babyhood, telling why that time was so special.

Write out your own birth announcement as it may have appeared in the newspaper.

Tell about the traits you inherited from your ancestors.

What is your star sign? What characteristics are you supposed to have according to the stars?

Cut out pictures from magazines which tell about your likes and dislikes. Add written comments to each picture.

Design your own personal crest!

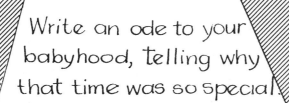

Spotlight on you

Christmas Capers

Redesign Father Christmas' suit to make it more suitable for the Australian climate.

Invent a supersonic sleigh!

Think of several different animals that could be useful to Santa during the time he is delivering the presents in Australia. Tell why each would be of use.

Write a job application to the manager of a large department store, stating why you would be perfect for the job of "Shop Santa", over the busy Christmas season.

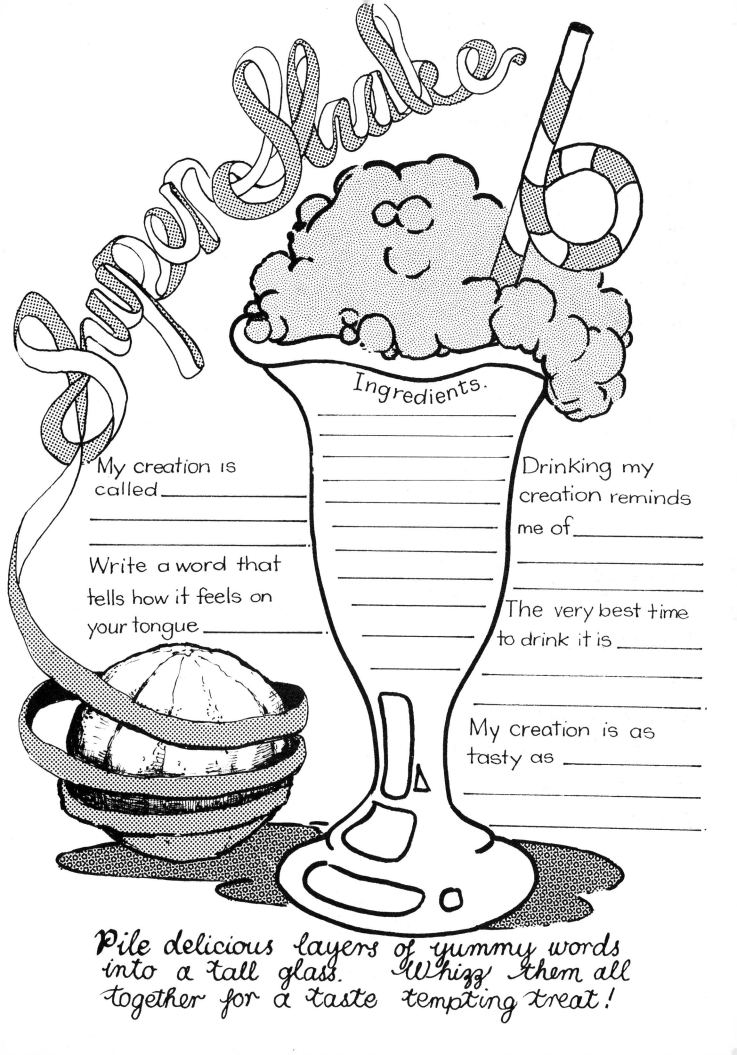

Super Shake

Ingredients.

My creation is
called _____
_____
_____

Write a word that
tells how it feels on
your tongue _____.

Drinking my
creation reminds
me of _____
_____
_____

The very best time
to drink it is _____
_____.

My creation is as
tasty as _____
_____

Pile delicious layers of yummy words
into a tall glass. Whizz them all
together for a taste tempting treat!

PRE-LOVED CARS

FOR SALE

List words that are used to attract attention.
3. 1.
4. 2.

What do these abbreviations mean?
s/roof.
Km.
reg.
immac. cond.
o.n.o.
air cond.

Locate several vehicles which are for sale. What techniques do the garages use to attract your attention?

Prepare your own used car ad. Sell off the family car or invent one of your own!

ON COMMERCIAL AIRLINES, EACH PILOT MUST EAT A DIFFERENT MEAL. THIS IS A GENERAL PRECAUTION TO ENSURE THAT IF ONE PILOT CONTRACTS FOOD POISONING, THE OTHER WILL STILL BE ABLE TO FLY THE PLANE SAFELY TO ITS DESTINATION.

- You and a friend are the two pilots.
- Write the evening's flight menu. (Choice of three main meals.)
- Act out the conversation with your co-pilot as you are deciding which dinner to choose.
- What happens if you both want the same?

Flight Number_____ Destination_____ Date_____

❧ Main Course for this Evening ❧
(a choice of three scrumptious dinners)

Item 1: _____

Item 2: _____

Item 3: _____

What's the Sense

Many ordinary things around us can be perceived differently simply by applying our sensory awareness.

1. How does sunshine smell?
2. Describe the sound of sizzling sausages.
3. What does chalk on the blackboard feel like?
4. How does yellow feel to you?

❧ <u>Invent a new vegetable.</u> ❧
  * What does it taste like?
  * Make up a recipe which incorporates your marvellous new vegetable.
  * How should it be cooked and served?

Artline 70
HIGH PERFORMANCE

Holidaze!

1. List the most fashionable items you'll need to pack for a holiday to:
   i) a ski resort
   ii) a healthy slimming farm.
   iii) a planet in another galaxy.
   iv) an archaeological site.
   v) an underground cave

2. You are having a holiday at _____.
(select anywhere you like real or imaginary).
Write a letter to a friend telling what you are seeing and doing.

3. You have inherited a tropical isle or a mountain lodge (select one) from a relative who has just died. Think of 10 different ways to make your island/lodge especially appealing to holiday makers who love to get away from civilization, but not its comforts!

4. Prepare a simple advertising leaflet convincing people that this island/lodge is the best possible place for a unique holiday.

Bah! Think about how all these holiday makers are goin' to affect the locals!! Write a letter to the council.

FOOD FOR THOUGHT

Lemon

- Write one word which describes what the whole lemon looks like. (before cutting.)

- How does the outer skin feel? (1 word)

- Now with your own piece of lemon, suck in the juice ... (no cheating!)

- What is your first reaction?

- What happens to your tongue?

- How do your teeth feel?

- Describe other feelings, quickly jot them down!

HISTORICAL FLOUR MILL BUILT N.1855

Old Flour Mill. Greenough.

You have some overseas visitors coming to stay with you. They hope to be in your area for at least a few days ...

1. <u>Select</u> 5 places you would recommend that they visit.

2. <u>Select</u> 5 places you would definitely not recommend they visit.

3. <u>Plan</u> two days of sightseeing. Set out a timetable to include :
   i   places to visit
   ii   how much time to be spent at each place.
   iii type of transport you would be using.

4. <u>Design</u> a newspaper ad. for a local scenic spot.

SCENIC TOURS INC.

secret messages

(1.) Paint a message with a small brush onto paper with either orange juice, lemon juice, vinegar or milk

- Send it to a friend, asking him or her to meet you at a special place.
- Mention the time and where you'll be waiting.
- Let the paper dry.

  Your friend can hold the message near a hot light bulb or the surface of a hot iron or in very hot sunlight, to decipher the message you've written.

(2.) Place a sheet of waxed paper over ordinary writing paper. Using a pencil, press hard and write a secret message in reply to your friend.

* To read the message, your friend must brush a wash of thin watercolour over the page. The waxy printing resists the colour and the message can easily be read.

PSSSSTT.!!

USE A SPECIAL CODE NAME FOR YOURSELF AND YOUR FRIEND.
[JUST IN CASE YOU ARE DISCOVERED!]

Interviewing Technique

An interviewer asks questions which do not require a yes or no answer. The questions asked encourage the person being interviewed to answer in sentences explaining in detail his or her thoughts.

Here are some of the types of questions asked. Complete the sentences.

What happened when _____ ?

Where were you during _____ ?

Why did _____ ?

Can you remember when _____ ?

How do you feel about _____ ?

What about _____ ?

What do you think will _____

Please tell our listeners exactly _____

ON THE AIR!

Manufacturers use many carefully planned and clever ways to capture our attention and to persuade us of the excellence of their products. Advertisers use the language of _persuasion_ to interest the potential buyer.

The class is divided into groups.

Each group must invent a _secret_ _product_ (the products must all be the same type of product, eg. all different sorts of soft drink, or different types of soap powder.)

(1. _Design_ an eye catching label for your product.

(2. _Design_ a whole advertising campaign, _writing_ a radio jingle, and _acting_ out a television commercial.

Interviews

Look at the list of interview subjects. Select someone to interview you. Before you act out the interview, get together for a few minutes to work out some of the questions & responses.

Interview Subjects

1. The Prime Minister.
2. A stuntman after completing a dangerous act.
3. A famous sportsperson.
4. A lifesaver who has just rescued someone.
5. An actor or actress in a television show.
6. A sea captain whose ship has sunk.
7. A pilot whose plane was hijacked.
8. A well known rock singer.
9. A victim of a kidnap after your release.
10. A bank manager after an armed hold up.

- Design a record cover.
- Write a title for the album and list each of the songs.
- What's the name of the person or Group making this recording?
- Describe the type of person who would be likely to buy this record.
- Write a review of this album as it might appear... in a rock magazine or as a segment on a television show.

Flip a disc!

Think of five completely different uses for this record disc!

You have found a tape which has accidentally been left in the phone box by a mysterious stranger. You replay the tape and discover what it reveals...

TREES

Write 5 good reasons for trees!

<u>List</u> 10 words to describe how a tree feels:
* during a high wind.
* on a hot, sunny day.
* As the neighbourhood kids climb in the branches

Do a bark rubbing.

<u>Write</u> a short speech that will explain how to <u>climb</u> a tree (to someone who's never done it.)

<u>Create</u> a delicious, nutritious, healthy food-tree. Cut pictures of healthy foods from magazines & glue them onto the branches of a sturdy tree you've drawn.

Make a <u>Class Tree Directory</u>. Draw, label and describe the particular characteristics of a tree special to you.

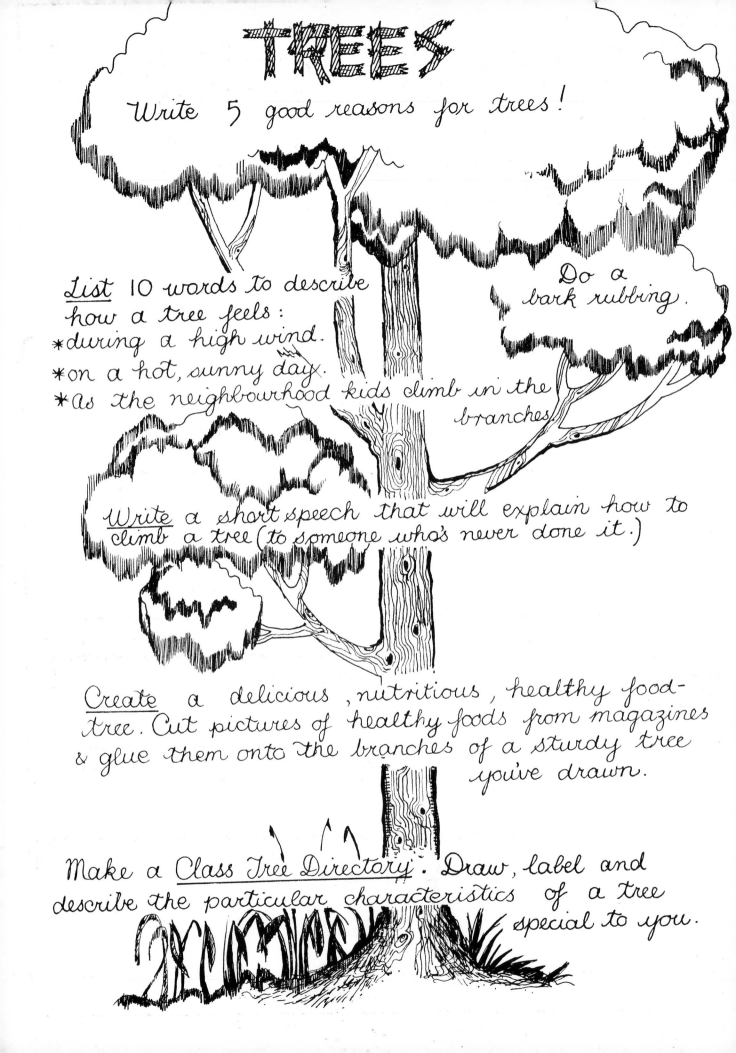

DRAW UP YOUR OWN FAMILY TREE

I AM:

_____

born: _____

MY PARENTS ARE:

_____
born: _____

_____
born: _____

MY GRANDPARENTS ARE:

born: _____   born: _____   born: _____   born: _____

MY GREAT GRANDPARENTS ARE:

FINGERPRINT TYPES

PLAIN ARCH

ACCIDENTAL WHORL

TENTED ARCH

CENTRAL POCKET LOOP

DOUBLE LOOP

LOOP

PLAIN WHORL

Fingerprint Fun

RIGHT HAND

✳ *Record your own fingerprints by using the teacher's stamp pad!*

LEFT HAND

- <u>Create thumbprint characters</u>. Write down the conversations between your characters using speech bubbles.

- A detective wants to know what you did between 6pm and 8pm last night. Write down everything exactly as you remember it.

Time Warp

You are a creature who has arrived from out of time.
What's your name? _____
What era have you come from?

_____

Give your description of a toaster, a set of traffic lights or a washing machine; imagine that you are seeing the object for the first time.

_____
_____
_____
_____
_____

* You are a reporter who has been sent to interview this strange being from out of time. Describe its appearance, and prepare ten interesting questions to ask him.

Remarkable cake mixture

CHOC-O-LOSSO

RELAX! It's so..o..o... Simple!

1. **PREHEAT** oven to 180°C or 350°F
2. **GREASE** tin(s) and line bottom(s) with paper.
3. **BLEND** this wonderfully simple mixture with an egg and 150 ml cold water.
4. **BEAT** at top speed for 1 minute.
5. **BAKE** 20 cm x 8cm oblong tin for 40-45 mins; or two 15 cm tins for 30-35 minutes.
6. **DECORATE** to your heart's desire.

DECORATION IDEA: "Smoothe" on lashings of clotted cream, add chunky slices of marshmallow and strawberries!!

- If I am using only one tin, how long will the cake take to cook? _____, at what temperature °C?_____.

- How would you improve this recipe? _____

_____

_____

- List 2 ingredients the powdered mix would be likely to contain. _____ and _____

- *Imagine you are the manufacturer of CHOC-O-LOSSO, what are the terms of the guarantee?

- *Say in one sentence why your cake mix is the best on the market. _____

_____

_____

- Draw & describe your version of the finished cake.

Bananarama Pty. Ltd.

- <u>Design</u> a trademark for the new Bananarama Company.

- <u>Create</u> a banana design for a new range of paper cups, paper plates and picnic napkins.

How many sides does a banana have?

- <u>Write</u> a bumper sticker, encouraging people to eat more bananas.

- <u>Make</u> up an advertising jingle for the same purpose.

- <u>Give</u> 5 reasons why bananas with zippers will soon be all the rage!

- <u>Dream</u> up a deliciously different dessert. Draw it. Describe it.

- Make a list of jobs which will be required by this new Company.

- From your list, choose one that may suit you.

- Write a resumé of yourself, telling why you are the best person for the job.

- Design an application form for one of the jobs. This will be given to prospective employees to fill out. State what specific tasks the employee will be expected to do.

- A conversation is taking place between the Manager of the Company and an employee. The boss is angry that his employee is being lazy and suggests that he rapidly improves if he wants to keep the job. Record exactly what is said!

... SOCK PUPPETS

What You Need : Sock , wool , cotton, felt patches, needle, buttons and material scraps.

What You Do : Sew a piece of felt between the toe and heel of the sock. This acts as the mouth. Buttons and other features can be sewn on.

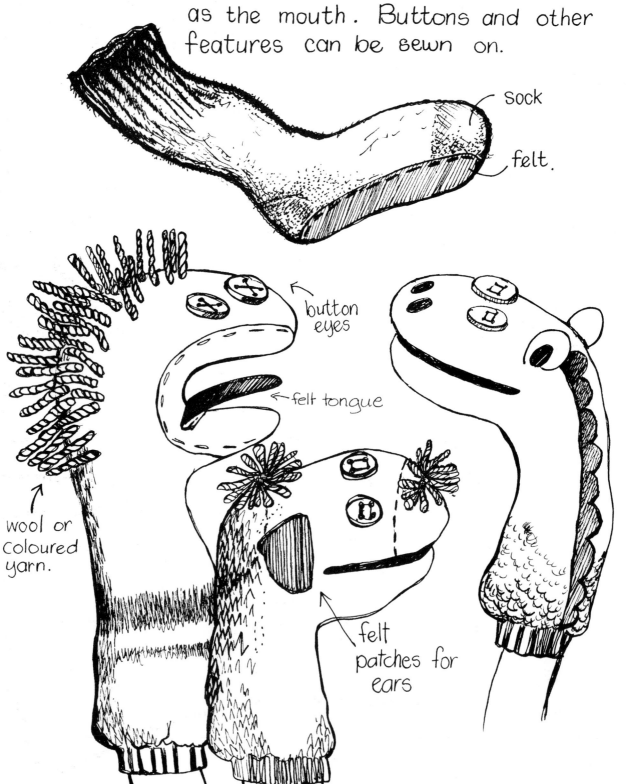

sock

felt.

button eyes

felt tongue

wool or coloured yarn.

felt patches for ears

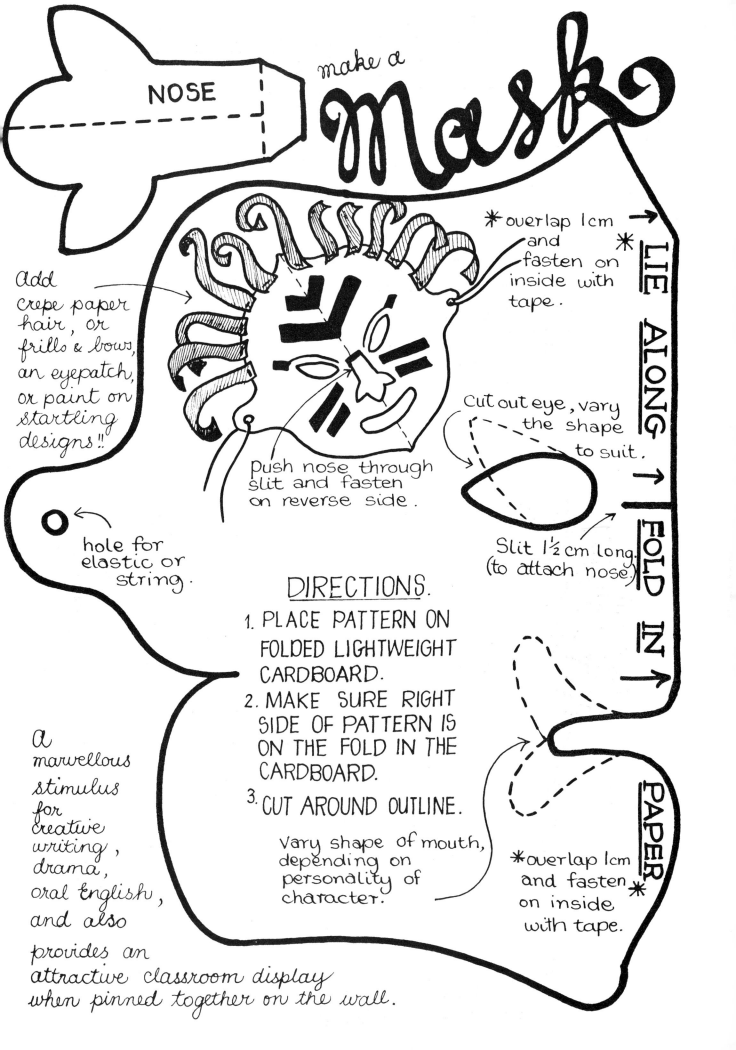

NOSE

make a **Mask**

Add crepe paper hair, or frills & bows, an eyepatch, or paint on startling designs !!

* overlap 1cm and fasten on inside with tape.

LIE ALONG

Cut out eye, vary the shape to suit.

push nose through slit and fasten on reverse side.

Slit 1½ cm long. (to attach nose)

hole for elastic or string.

FOLD IN

DIRECTIONS.

1. PLACE PATTERN ON FOLDED LIGHTWEIGHT CARDBOARD.
2. MAKE SURE RIGHT SIDE OF PATTERN IS ON THE FOLD IN THE CARDBOARD.
3. CUT AROUND OUTLINE.

Vary shape of mouth, depending on personality of character.

A marvellous stimulus for creative writing, drama, oral English, and also provides an attractive classroom display when pinned together on the wall.

PAPER

* overlap 1cm and fasten on inside with tape.

Draw an animal who is bigger than a mouse, has long pointed ears, a curly tail, large glinting eyes, sharp teeth, and is covered with shaggy hair

One reason I would like to be

_____ is because:
name of animal

_____
_____

Write a lunch or dinner invitation from your animal to the zoo keeper.

Write directions for how to capture this animal if it ever manages to escape.

Zoo Doings

Write a letter to an animal you'd like to convince to be your pet.

IF, THROUGH CIRCUMSTANCES, YOU HAD TO LIVE WITH A GROUP OF ANIMALS, WHICH TYPE OF ANIMAL WOULD YOU CHOOSE? WHY?

REWARD

MAKE UP A POSTER describing an animal that is missing from the zoo. Tell about the animal's appearance, suggest types of places the animal may be heading for. Does the animal have a name? Is there a reward offered?

The Crazy Class Book of Guiness Records

Present yourself as a fabulous
Super hero or a Spectacular
Record breaker, an incredible
Genius or a special V.I.P!

Write about what makes you so special

REMARKABLE!

You are the world's most famous
Sporting personality. At which
sport do you excel? What
special training programme
do you follow? Tell us the
secret of your amazing success

Tell about three or four things that have made you laugh

This kookaburra's
name is <u>Tatterback</u>.
• Think of a suitable
name to call his,
mother _____
brother _____ .
friend _____ .
father _____ .

• Compile a
list of
humorous
words!

• Think of five different reasons why Tatterback
could be laughing. Write them down.
• How do <u>you</u> think kookaburras got their laugh?

United Kingdom   AUSTRALIA   UNITED STATES

people with passports

Using the format below, design a passport for:

a) <u>Seymour Clearly.</u> ~ famous scientist and inventor of the amazing bionic bifocal spectacles.

b) <u>Troy D'Aulatt.</u> ~ international con man and part-time secret agent.

c) <u>Sugar Devine.</u> ~ gorgeous, glamorous fashion model.

d) <u>Your own self.</u>

DESCRIPTION

NAME	
PLACE & DATE OF BIRTH	

HEIGHT	**COLOUR OF EYES**
COLOUR OF HAIR	**VISIBLE PECULIARITIES**

CHILDREN

Name	Place & Date of birth.	Sex

Issued at _____

on........._____

and valid for (5) years from that date

signed by _____

(An officer duly authorized under Section 7 of the Passports Act 1938-1973)

_____

PHOTOGRAPH OF BEARER.   SIGNATURE OF BEARER

PASSPORT TO ADVENTURE

Your passport is the key which enables you to visit and explore new countries. Use it to experience different cultures and lifestyles.

Design a travel brochure which will arouse the interest and enthusiasm in fellow travellers.

Include these details in your brochure.

1. What type of climate and terrain can be expected.
2. What travellers will need to take with them (eg. warm woolly jumpers? climbing boots? bathers?)
3. What type of accommodation is available and the types of local food.
4. The cost and the best way of getting there.

Fold your paper into interesting and different shapes before you start.

Fast Food

Should fast food be sold?
Write an answer to this question from the point of view of:
1. A health food fanatic.
2. A 12 year old person.
3. The mother of this person.
4. A doctor.
5. The manager of McDonalds.

Compile The "Complete Guide to Eating Hamburgers!"

Create your own fast food outlet.
• What is the name of your business?
• What foods do you specialize in?
• Make up a catchy advertising slogan for T.V & radio.
• What sort of uniform will be worn by your staff?

• Describe five burgers other than hamburgers!
• What makes fast food so fast?

Royal Mail

- Design a stamp for one of the following ...
  1. An important sporting event.
  2. A well known man or woman.
  3. A fabulous festival.
  4. A unique land feature.
  5. Your own city or town.

- This stamp will one day be a collectors item, tell about what makes it so special.

- Write a short & snappy stamp poem. Begin the first line with S, the second with T, third with A, etc.

- A person who collects stamps is a _____.

PEOPLE PROFILES

1. From the list, select one person. Write a letter from this person to any other person on the list. It can be a letter of complaint, a congratulatory letter, a query, a mail order or any sort of letter you like.

2. <u>Select</u> a different person from the list. Build up a character profile of this person, what he/she likes, dislikes, what he/she thinks is important in life, ambitions etc. 3. <u>Write</u> diary entries for a week for this person (as you think this person might write it.)

doctor	Principal	typist
dentist	rubbish collector	surfer
teacher	bank manager	chauffeur
plumber	station master	aerobics instructor
artist	shop assistant	jockey
schoolboy	cleaner	accountant
schoolgirl	mechanic	scientist
university student	old age pensioner	sailor
prime minister	newspaper editor	zookeeper
carpenter	migrant	politician
cook	reporter	fireman
butcher	health inspector	nurse
baker	electrician	musician
hypnotist	builder	sales person
tramp	sportsman	tea lady
rock singer	chemist	clairvoyant
film star	fisherman	actor
disc jockey	coalminer	parking attendant
gambler	beach inspector	air hostess
clown	author	farmer

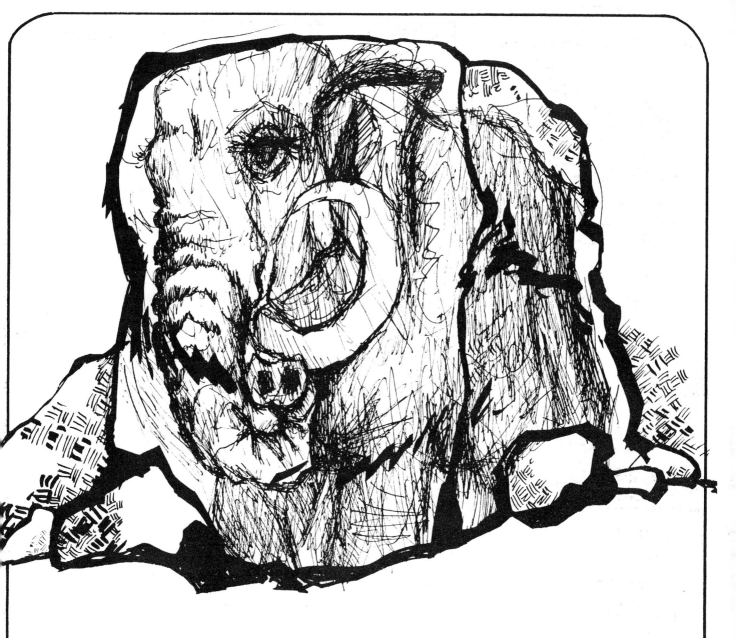

A creature has remained frozen
within a solid block of ice for
thousands of years.

Slowly the ice is beginning to melt.

- What is eventually revealed ?

- What is its first reaction ?

- Write what will happen next !

RED HOT IDEAS

- Write 2 questions you would like to ask a pizza maker. If you were a pizza maker, what 2 questions would you be sure to ask the customer?

- Unscramble these pizza words: 1) roomshum.
    2) eesche.
    3) hillice.
    4) nooni.
    5) reeng reppep.

- Create your own red hot, spicy pizza. Decide how you are going to sell it to your customers.

- Design a brochure showing how scrumptious your pizzas are, and lots of different ways to eat them.

- Think up 5 interesting uses for a frozen pizza!

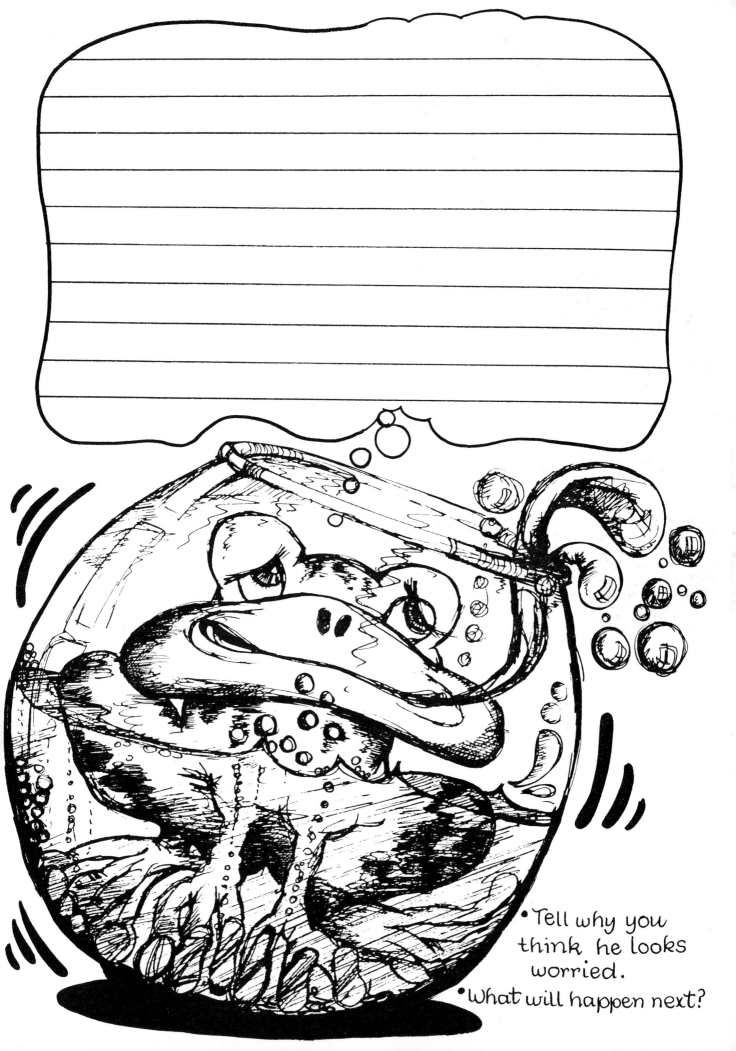

• Tell why you think he looks worried.
• What will happen next?

Explain how to cut a beard and moustache off someone who is asleep.

Write diary entries containing feelings, thoughts & experiences of the first few hours of the hatchling's life...

Write the first words it utters...

_____
_____
_____
_____
_____
_____
_____
_____

Write out a birth certificate for the new hatchling.

Complete its thoughts,

I may appear to be _____
_____

but really I am _____
_____

I am talented at _____
_____

but not so good at _____
_____

Tune In

- Create a song about how to give a haircut.

- Make up a new verse for a song you already know.

- Write a jingle for a new breakfast cereal or sandwich spread.

Write a _convincing_ letter to your teacher, telling why this frog would make the ideal classroom pet.

Write what she is saying to the dog!

What is the dog thinking?

Here is a yawn.

Describe what happens when you yawn.

A hiccup.

How does a hiccup happen?